BOOK BENCHERS

PUBLICATIONS

PRESENTS

A Weird life

Compiled By

S. Harshanadevi

AELAY PUBLICATION

A dream come true for every writers out there. We spot every possible problem for the writers, help in rectifying them and guide them towards the best outcome. We make sure to understand your needs, dreams and expectations, and nourish them with our services and stop not until we fulfill your dreams. The writers have a right and freedom to choose what they want here. They have us to guide them through the hardest path until the end. Believe in us.

Aelay Publication - by a writer for the writers.

BOOK BENCHERS

Book Benchers is the affiliate of Aelay publication. Both the publication is handled by Astro.
Aelay plays the role of publishing solo books.
And Book Benchers is epically for publishing anthologies.

Book Benchers have 2 different teams.
1. Tamil

2. English/Hindi

Never mind what our main motive is to help all the budding writers, who are seeking for their dream of publishing their own book to come true.

We are there to help out everyone.
In guiding for starting up with your carrier in compiling until finishing up your full book.

<u>COPYRIGHT</u>

First Edition: October 2021

Design And Executed by

 **aelay Publish**.com

ISBN : 978-93-91423-85-8

Page : 115

<u>ACKNOWLEDGEMENT</u>

To list who all have helped us is difficult because they are so numerous and the depth is so enormous. We would like to acknowledge the following as being idealistic channels and fresh dimensions in the completion of this book.
We take this opportunity to thank the Co-authors for being a part of this book and submitting their beautiful writer-ups and making this book more special.
We would like to thank the publication team for providing the necessary facilities required for the completion of this book. We take this opportunity to thank our book editor for the moral support and guidance.
Lastly, We would like to thank every person who directly or indirectly helped me in the completion of the book especially my parents and peers who supported me throughout my book.

<u>DISCLAIMER</u>

This Anthology is a work of fiction. Our editors have tried their best to avoid any sort of plagiarism and the proof-readers have done their job of proofreading best on their part to expertise the book with unplagiarized and original content. Still if any appropriation detected, the editorial team is no where responsible, the author is solely responsible for such acts. We have well guided our co-authors to submit their original write-ups.

FOUNDER

IRUDAGA ASTRO

Irudaga Astro, From Tirunelveli, Founder of
Aelay and BB (Book Benchers)
He had completed his BE.
He has written 3 Tamil poetry book's which
hits the top list on social media!
His main aim is to allow the writers to
publish their words as their book rather than
just Posting them on Insta.

LINK AND POSTER MAKER

CATHERINE ASMI T

Catherine Asmi T, From Tirunelveli
She has completed her M.com
Her passion is Drawing and Designing.

TEAM HEAD

She is a passionate writer from Chennai. Writing makes her pressure go away. She had played the role of co-author for more than 100+ Antho's. She would like to thank her parents and her Loveable Brother for supporting her rather than stopping her from what she wanted to do! For being the main reason for achieving her dreams. As well as for standing beside her in all the ups and downs. Whenever she feels like she needs to get out of her stressful timing or feels like she needs peacefulness, she starts to paint, she would never mind sitting in the same place for so many hours when it comes to her painting. She believes that anyone could hurt her, But never her books could!!

Catch her in Insta and FB
Insta: @theinnocentheart
FB: KA. PARINASRI

<u>INDEX</u>

19. Navina. G

20. SRIJA SADHUKHAN

21. Deesha Soni

22. B.S.KRISHNAN

23. Samira Rahman

24. Debangana Dutta

25. Priya Singh

26. N. Krishnaveni

27. Lalithaa S S

28. M.Srinithi

29. Ajeeba Jahan A

30. Nirudhi N.R

31. S.T. Renuka

32. Mohini Keshri

33. Banupriya K

34. Vishnupriya S

35. Ajitha Gulnas J

36. T R SRI VIDYA APARNA

37. Durga Balamadhavan

38. Sumathi palanisamy

39.RamadeviChelliah

40.Kajal Chaudhary

41.Jebisha

42.ATHIRA CK

43.ShanmugaPriya.T

44.Prachi Gupta

45. SrijitaSaha

46.K.Prathik

47.Mohamed Sathik M

48.Raja Boovendran. P

49.Kousika Moorthi

50.Saurabh SantGyaneshwarKhobragade

A Weird life

COMPILER

She is Harshana from Ramanathapuram, Tamil
Nadu. She completed her Masters in English. She
loves to explore something new. She has more
passion in innovating new ides. She was sportive
and humour. She loves to be happy always. She has
many friends and love to make new friends. Her
dream is to be different.

Weird

Sometimes weird is good

It will show who we are

It's not a bad thing

To curse

It's a wonderful thing

We never feel it

Once

We try to understand

What is weird

We'll never be common

Try to find out your

Utkarsh Jain

Utkarsh Jain is writer poet who writes & romanticizes the beauty of everything around him into his words & makes it feel alive. He is from pusad, Maharashtra.

Insta id: utkarshjain19

"Youth and Emotions…"

Youth is like a storehouse of ebullience, energy and
emotions
It's youth that decides
the shape of the future of its nation

He wandered in the streets of stranger where every
eye stared at him
thinking he have lost his way
But he have lost his faith from the promises of the
world

He have been wanting
To spend time alone
Amidst the crowd of unknown..

So Full of deceit
His Life's a contradiction
One day it's reality
The next one is fiction

DHARSHINI. M

She is Dharshini from kovilpatti. She is pursing masters in English. She has huge interest in writing. she loves to share her thought and emotion through her writing. She has done many anthology as co author . She has published a book named 'vox of mine '.

Insta id: dharshji_dharsh

Life is weird

Sometimes life seems weird,

Not because only by bad things

Might be the longing of happiness

When our favourite person turns stranger

When our well-wishers demotivate us

And the loss of our beloved souls

Those stuffs hits hard

And made us

To look the life weird

All we need is strong heart

To tackle and cross the part

Life is weird !! It's happens !!

Anjali tomar

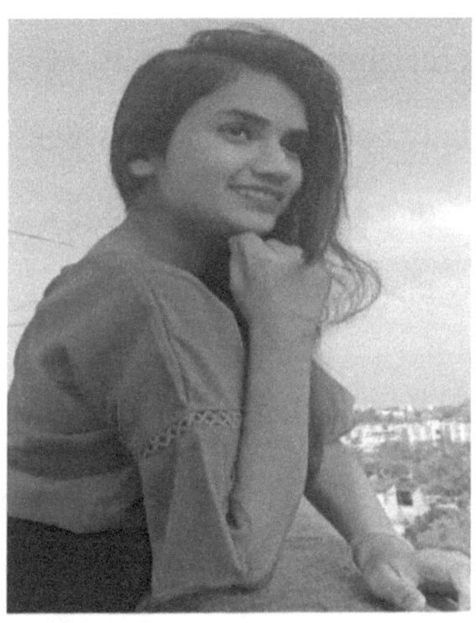

Hi, I m anjalitomar – writter and artist.

Student by a day and writer in the night. Writing is not my passion to follow as a career but when a opportunity knock my door I cant let it go. Recently I m working in a short story script which is not published yet. Basically I put love and aggression into words and help you connect with the people + moments that matter.

I m the mirror of this world who shows the real side always.

Insta id: Nagamaa_lafzo_k

Shitty claim…

Don't blame the girl to be raped,

This shitty claim she is wearing a skirt,

Don't proclaimed because u are a Great writer,

This shitty claim to shame to struggled writer,

Don't gain sympathy to be a girl,

This shitty claim that you are weak because you are female,

Don't came back to that person life who ditched you,

This shitty claim that because u love them,

Don't frame others in your own problems,

This shitty claim that because u cant handle your own problems,

Don't vain your talent because other don't want you to do that,

This shitty claim that u cant fight for tour own dreams,

Don't be same person forever because u were use to that personality,

This shitty claim that people don't accept the change in u and u cant bear that change in yourself….

Mohammed Niyaz

Mohammed Niyaz hails from Mumbai – The City Of Dreams. He often loves to write poetries and short music video stories for his own youtube channel. Apart from this Mohammed is currently working on his upcoming anthologies, as well writing poetries since 2013. You can find him on facebook/mohammedniyaz as well on instagram @niyazsks.

Quote

1. Monsoon has arrived now with loads of happiness.

Moments of cherished has been on the way of laughter.

Paper boats has been sailing through the water ways.

With each and every time children's good day.

2. The sky has called out for the clouds.

With sounds of thunderstorms around.

Round and round the lightning strikes again.

Rain rain come again with few drops of hope insane.

3. Winds stood by the seasons greetings.

When climatic conditions became surprisingly beautiful.

Sign of presence was seen in the atmosphere.

When sudden grounds of numerous occasions saved.

Krishna moorthy

Krishna Moorthy was born in Madurai, Tamil Nadu. Growing up, he was fascinated with cricket and this interest led to some early exposure to reading since he was drawn to stories related to adventures. He was a script writer for the ELA during his final year in college.

Insta Id: Arvind krishnamoorthy

Cooper's drive in, foot-hills of Kodai

I live a happy life, indeed a very happy one, Still there are parts of my conscious which search for the damozel.

I search for us in the time stamps we left far behind We were young and naïve.

Mr Gaur has died a year ago, Nala,the cook, has long gone to Manipur, Mr Narayan tha bottle painter went back to Udupi years ago.

I came here to find us 3 years ago .

Har Deepansh Bahadur Sinha

He is HarDeepanshBahadur Sinha .He belongs to Lucknow,UP. He is a research scholar of Oceanography and has done masters in Geography from National Post Graduate College. Completed his schooling from Study Hall.His hobbies are art , listening to music , cooking & loads of driving. His interest areas are Astronomy, Writing, Photography & Travelling a lot.

Insta id: Deepansh_sinha

A Nineties Era

It was a period full of calmness

Where every moment brought happiness,

No mobile no tablets but only talks

I still miss those lovely night walks.

When siblings got united during vacations

It reflected chemistry as well as dedication,

Whether it's an indoor or outdoor game

We enjoyed it without a bit of shame.

Nobody has got car neither knows driving

But the real pleasure came from cycling,

We stocked beautiful colorful kites

For that we did numerous fights .

No malls no cafes no restaurants

Yet we did loads of enjoyment,

Today we are approaching towards thirties

Still we are lost somewhere in nineties.

Singing dancing painting was our speciality

Cooking stitching was also in our qualities,

Though we not had grand celebrations

Towards family we had immense devotion.

Harshita Verma

Co-author HarshitaVerma is a writer from Lucknow. She has completed her graduation in commerce stream. She has been writing poetry for the last few years as her passion. She wants to be a novelist in future.

Insta id: 0___hsh

Rain love

The black sky and the cold air

The rain drops making nature fair

The environment so peaceful

The smell of the soil wet with water

Felt only during the rains

The rain falling on everything

With no discrimination of any sort

Getting wet in the rain

Intensifies the love for this season

Enjoying each moment of the rains

Spreading a different light

The heat of the summer lost

The rain heavy or a drizzle

Brings a colour to the nature

Making mind filled with peace

Madhumitha

A conscious dreamer letting her thoughts out through pen and paper

Insta id: Feel.Free.Fun.24

Bad luck

It's just a game of time,

Won't be permanently yours or mine,

Bad luck is just a phase of life,

When at rest are the positive vibes.

Now we wonder every moment,

Why things at times go worst?

Have we ever thought?

These are our past deeds' result.

Win and lose are two forms only,

Why do you take defeat so deeply?

Just keep in mind not at heart,

Time keeps on revolving again and again,

Don't be so hurt.

Tasneem Sheikh

Tasneem Sheikh of Assam, author of '**Tulips Coffee and You**', is a 17 year old poet and writer, co-author of 80 anthologies and numerous magazines. She was recognized as a young achiever in English Literature by esteemed personalities of Maria's Montessori in 2016. A critic, counsellor and humanitarian, apart from her endearment for literature, she also holds a passion towards music, expressive artwork, creativity and adventures.

Instagram: la_nuit_portrait

VENTURE

We cried and wailed, for something to soothe the
penetrating injection

We joined school, we laughed.

Fell into tears, danced more in colours

The petals bloomed, naïve and soft.

We grew up, learned how the balance works;
Happiness and pain

Like a pendulum, swinging in breeze.

We fell deeper, got up, fell twice harder

The petals persisted the stormy winters.

Realized how a piece of cake brings joy following
a truck-load of troubles.

Life gave more pain than the needles, we learnt to
smile at it with ease.

The clock struck twelve,

Faded, the petals withered away.

A Weird life

Lipsa Dabhi

She is Author and also good Co-Author. She is eighteen years old, she is student of the computer engineering.She is extraordinary person. She is always good leader. Her mam mrunalprajapati is her inspiration person and also her motivater, her friend chetnaraval also supported to her and her mom manisha ben and her father nileshbhai also supported to her for anytype of her creativity.

She also wrote poems, short stories, shayries.

Her writing skills almost very well and her creative collections are always best.

Insta id: __lipsa__dabhi__0829

" Life "

Life is not a simple but life is unique,

Life in stay with positivity,

Because of positivity is good part of life,

And also good thoughts of life,

With positivity life is perfect,

Life is one and only best part of life,

Life also very wonderful and beautiful,

Only who understood life's rules who satisfaction
with life struggles,

Life is extraordinary so enjoy life with extra beauty,

Life is natural not a critical,

Life is faithful and hopeful,

Life is enjoy with happiness and love,

Because life is wonder and special.

Jasmine Panda

Miss Jasmine Panda is presently pursuing Ph.D. Chemistry from Ravenshaw University, Odisha, India. She is a Gold Medalist and University Topper in her B.Sc. and M.Sc. She has completed an internship CSIR-SRTP in IICT Hyderabad. She holds the post of Senate Member of the University for the session 2019-20 in Academic Pursuits. She is a Governor Awardee for Youth Red Cross. She has received All-Rounder Award in her 12th standard for excellence in extracurricular activities along with studies. She is a Topper throughout her career. She has been Literary and Cultural Champion in her college days. She has also cracked a campus in Vedanta. She has hosted in numerous events including International events and has been appreciated as an anchor.

Insta id: jas_writes05

Old is Gold

Clinging on to the memories that went,

Magical were the unforgettable moments spent!

Challenging that time the ongoing trends,

Amazing was the journey with friends!

Combo of our naughtiness and elder's strictness,

Catering to our physical and mental wellness!

Peaceful were those lovely school time rhymes,

Historic were our childish notorious crimes!

The fun in those school and college days,

The movies that time, typical in their ways!

Enjoying to the fullest every season,

Attempting to do all kinds of fusion!

Those times were really the best,

Seriously missing those aromas, those taste!

Leaving so far our memorable childhood,

Really, it's rightly said that "Old is Gold".

Subha.V

I am Subha doing my B.A English final year. I personally love to write poems and quotes because of the journey I have been travelling since the 1st year of my college. I feel really grateful and joyous while writing this as it brings out my real admiration on things and its beauty. Thankful for this opportunity because these things made my lockdown days little blissful and happiest.

Insta id: Shravana27

SMILE

A powerful dosage of Happiness,

Positivity and Maturity.

Smile when you know yourself,

When you lose yourself,

And when you get back yourself..!!

Because

All these flaws need a curve

Which is supposed to be your smile.

The only free therapy

Which holds you and your surroundings

Delightful..!!

Flower blossoms when sunlight falls on it,

Soul speaks when smile plays over it.

Never crave for external beauty

Because,

You already deserved it by your smile.

Aarushi Giria

This is AarushiGiria, a 16 year old poet who has a perspective which she doesn't refrain from sharing with the world. Finds joy in smelling new books, the feeling of wind in the hair and barely taking 10 to make a poem. That being said, she's also just a teen using her passion to be vocal.

Insta id:verse.iom

CAN YOU EVER BE ALONE?

You can never be alone.

Look above, there's a sky,

Look at your right, there's a tree,

Look at your left, there's some bushes,

Look down, there's earth.

You can never be alone.

Look above, there are clouds ,

Look at your right, there are birds,

Look at your left, there are butterflies,

Look down, there are a million ants.

You can never be alone.

Look above, there's nature,

Look at your right, there's nature,

Look at your left, there's nature,

Look below, there's nature.

Kalamkaar

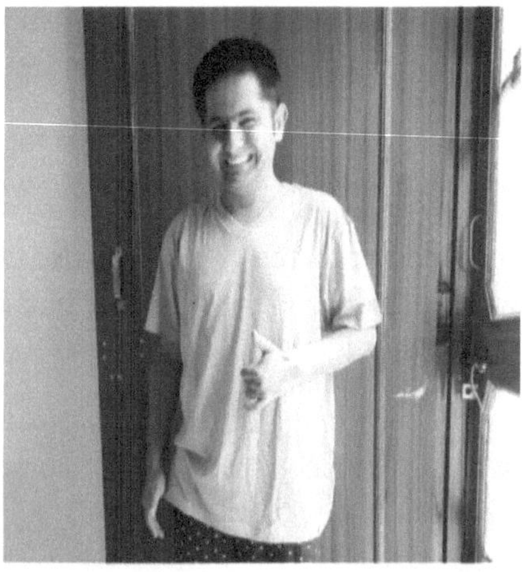

This is Kalamkaar. He is from Uttrakhand bought up in Meerut(Up). His hobbies are reading and writing. His interest is in writing. He love writing. He is part of 870+Anthologies as Co-Author. He won 740+ Certificate in Writing, He Start writing 28 February 2020. He is part of 13 anthology as Co Author going for record and He is omg record holder as Co -Author of Book Called Laposia. He is simple and people observer. His insta handle is kalamkaar51 and e-mail kalamkaar51@gmail.com. He believes in Karma.

Insta id: Kalamkaar5

Miss u a lot Poomi

Animals are all important don't hurt them.Love the animal, do not make them suffer.

If you ever meet in the dagger, then for your entertainment, do not go on beating them with stones.

Show them affection and care, they are also creatures, do not show curiosity. Keep them in your home and treat them like family members.

Show them affection and care, they are also creatures, do not show curiosity. Keep them in your home and treat them like family members.

When we were younger, we came with you.

We had brought gifts of happiness. You make a jump, but now if you don't then these things will not happen again. I miss you dear! I sleep under my bed. If I were alone, you would always be with me, do not let anything happen to me.

Take care of me and always play with me. I miss you, Poumi! Played with me, you would catch my leg while doing it.

Did not let go anywhere and in hide and seek, you would hide behind trees. I used to run in my voice, come to me! No one plays with me.

Lack will do your best. Who do you remember, I love you.

Anugrakhaa

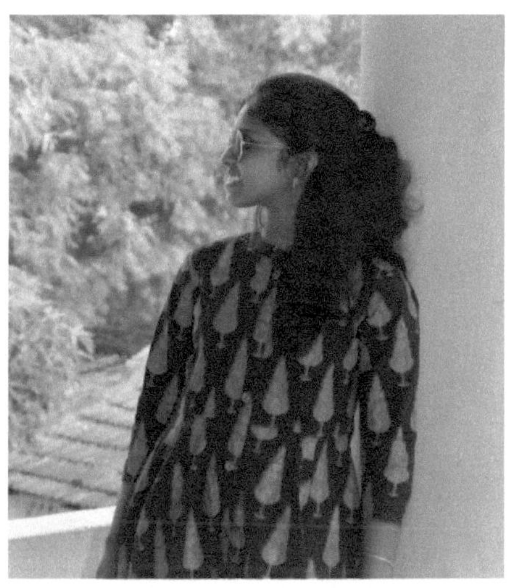

Holding Bachelors in English, pursuing Masters in Political science

Wandering, aspiring & striving to see hope & smile on vulnerable sections

Insta id: Anu002

I'm 70%

I host 80%

I recreate, regulate

Yet,

Today

I can't digest

I'm sick

I suffocate

Remember I'm 70%

Stop it further……

Yours care seeking

OCEAN

Berdhisha P

She is Berdhisha from Coimbatore. She loves to write poetry in Tamil and English. She is a blogger and you can see her poems in berdhisha96.blogspot.com . She is a co-author for about forty five Anthologies. She is a compiler too. She loves to travel and admire new things.

Insta id: thoughts_of_mine_the_muse

FRIEND – FOE

You think they are your friends,
They are not the real friends.

They spread a gentle smile,
They are dangerous blue whale.

Then talk as sweet as honey,
For them your life is just funny.

They look like a shining chain,
But, they are powerful bane.

You may help for them in danger,
They will make your life in danger.

When you stay away from fake friends,
Your life become as bright as the star.

Mohanapriya.K

Co-author Mohanapriya.K is a budding writer from Tamilnadu, India. She has completed her Bachelor's degree in Engineering stream. She has been a writer for one year as her passion. She wants to be a best compiler in future.

Instagram : @colours_honey_official

About Humanity

Truth is sometimes said to be oppressive.

Anything in the world can change over time but emotions alone will always remain the same within us.

Some emotions are always within us and we cannot hide them even though we think we should hide them.

What could be a creature without emotions!

In this heartfelt emotions are very important and essential.

Because many of us are walking the path of our heart, living by accepting what our heart says as scripture and as the master of our conscience.

Humanity is the best thing ever.

We must not give up humanity for anything.

ANKITA NAHAR

#AKII#@@@

AnkitaNahar, physically she live in AJMER, RAJASTHAN but heartly live in everywhere.

She is too much passionate about writing. She have always found comfort in words, and that's what attracts everyone.Writing is her therapy, she write what she feels and experiences in her life. You can take a look at her writings on Instagram @naharankita1

Yes I still remember

In rakhi gifts I get your

I'm afraid of you

And stare at you from afar

A new member came to the house

Name we gave him a selfie Was he so cute

Heart would fall on anyone

As much as he can in eating food Was it fun

The same as in the bath Death used to come

To take a shower Life used to leave us

Was part of my life

He was very intelligent

Nothing was spoken

But understood in gestures

Used to give all

On sight

Became a member of the household

Yes he became my life

© AKII # @@@

Navina. G

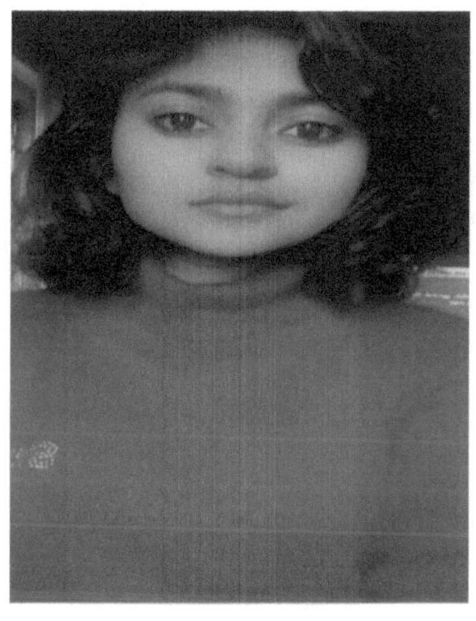

Scars are beautiful carvings..

Insta id: n_a.v.i.n_a

Luna Amor

She sits alone on the window sill,

And stares at him everyday,

How could he be so pale and still,

She realises sitting null.

Brighter than ever he is,

She wondered if he gave any attention,

And what could overtake this?

She thought at the moment's bliss.

As he cries without a word uttered,

She tries to rub away his tears,

But they seem to have all scattered,

All over the universe, they glittered.

The wolf on every full moon howls,

In extreme hunger of desperation,

While her heart let's a deep yowl,

Little did he know bout this wandering soul…

©Navina

SRIJA SADHUKHAN

SrijaSadhukhan is 19 years old girl studying BSc Biotechnology in Amity University Kolkata. Love to write poetry and a book worm too.

Insta id: Syncopatemysuccess

WEIRDO

Normalism has become a religion

That we keep realistic at bay,

Liking painful stories, moonless night

Deep conversation and hounds of wolves.

Ne"er let this world kill your hunger

Conquer each and every diverse goal we have,

We will be mostly weird and unsatisfied

To believe in the weird is to be an atheistic.

B.S.KRISHNAN

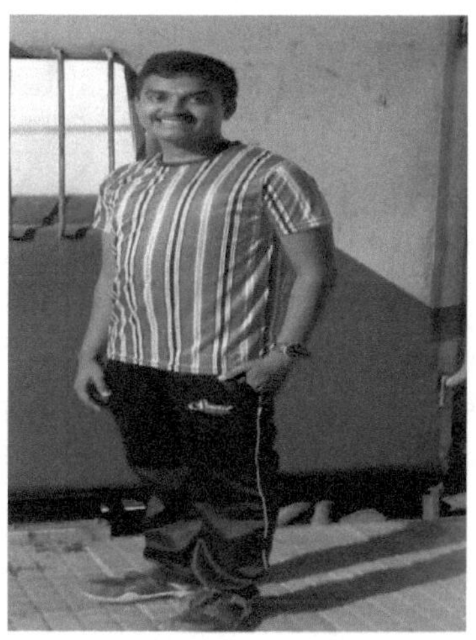

B.S.KRISHNAN . He is a 19 years old pursuing 2^{nd}B.Sc . He is from Erode, Tamilnadu. He is interested in writing both Tamil and English languages . He is also interested in Drawing . His hobbies are hearing music and do something with creative. You can search him on Facebook as B S Krishnan or on Instagram @ mathsbskrishnan002

QUOTES: (Lifeline)

"Do something for yourself with your own creation".

"Where there is a problem, there are solution to it".

"Teaching is not only getting from blackboard, it is getting from everywhere and everyone".

- B.S.KRISHNAN

A Weird life

Deesha Soni

DeeshaSoni..a Post Graduate and M.phil adorns the hat of a multitasker of an educationist,artist,poet,photographer,author , blogger,homemaker,wife and mother… She has 10 years experience in the field of Education as a Professor and Coordinator.Deesha has various publications to her credit ya national and international levels. Deesha has various published works to her credit… she has two books published on Amazon… named 'Just thoughts' and 'Random thoughts on pandemic'..Kindle edition and more than 100 plus published works on various online platforms of .. Deesha has also won many prizes in National and international levels in many write-ups…Deesha has also published her works in 235 plus anthologies of multiple genres…

Insta id: Deeshagauree

Every day the house turned into a battlefield, with heated arguments, abuses.,shifting blames and things being banged on floors. Toofan and his wife Sailaab were not coming to terms with each other. This lockdown had sneaked into trouble in paradise and their association of marriage seemed to be in the cracks. All this melodrama started a few days after the lockdown was announced. Initial days seemed to be quite a bliss, but as days passed by. This couple with 20 years of their marriage seemed it difficult to withstand each other's views, minute disagreements swelled into major squabbles… echoing their unpleasant fights… beyond the boundaries of the walls of their home… Had the lockdown made it tough for the twosome to stay under the same roof? These tiffs and brawls had now become a common subject in this house. One day amid the fight Toofan collapsed, his face turned pale and wet. Sailaab shrieked in horror and ran to the neighborhood doctor on the same floor. The physician interfaced that Toofan had suffered a mild attack. He instructed Sailaab to take utmost care of Toofan and prescribed medication.Day and night Sailaab was at her husband Toofan's aid and all the bitterness, fracas, quarrels vanished unexpectedly. Toofan silently admired Sailaab's selfless devotion for his welfare and safekeeping. Mutual hatred faded away and bloomed mutual understanding and love. Both Toofan and Sailaab realised how important they were for each other. How hard and unbearable grief would it be if either of them suffered a life threat, made an exit.

Samira Rahman

Samira Rahman is from Dhaka, Bangladesh. She is currently working at a financial institution, and to unwind herself, she works with her words every now and then.

Insta id: samira.rahman666

She tried.

The weigtage of those two words still feel heavy like a stone over my dead heart as I write it. She tried to maintain the balance – The Balance that was never in sync as she realized later. Didn't she try to hold the sails of the broken ship that was lost before it reached the mid sea? Her life didn't get to last with the crashing waves when it was the time. The promises with him were all like the foams of the waves, that when once lapped on the sands of the shore, got all soaked up. They didn't remain there anymore, like ceasing to exist.

And the worst, she believed on those transient foams of his vows and tried to keep the show going.

What was in it for her, anyway? What's in the lost hopes of a man who's dying an inevitable death? Her high yet consoling hopes were just that that led her towards her own demise. Yet her heart needed a little more boost to go through another day, pushed her to the brink of the end of the road. She did reach the end, whatever you call it – her last strand. Then the thread got broken.

Yes, she gave her best, only to be led to a painful fall, that left her in a life of a living dead. The futile attempts were all in vain. Yes, she tried only to reach her own death – the eternal misery of her own life's downfall.

A Weird life

Debangana Dutta

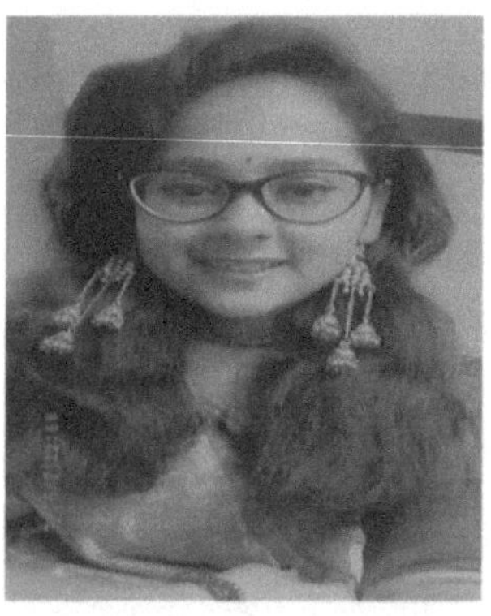

Hello, I am DebanganaDutta,daughter of Mitali and Dipankar Dutta. Right now, I am studying in Class 12. It was very early in my life when I realized writing is my true passion and since then I haven't looked back. My pen has been my constant companion, in times both good and bad. I am a logophile in the true sense of the word, and I sincerely hope my honest passion would be reflected in my work. I am very pleased to be in this world of Anthology and it would give me immense joy if my writings bring solace to all the people out there.According to me, writing isn't a work or job, it's the most genuine form of expressing what we actually feel. A book is a dream we hold in our hands.I want to let this dream create my own reality.

Insta id: @_._bubble_poetry_.

•Room•

Just wait for a second,

Let me organise the cluttered mess,

Definitely,

There is room for more.

For pens in pen stand.

Stacked. Stuffed.

For rays near shadows.

For those flowers in vase.

For painting on these walls.

There is room for more.

For thoughts in my mind.

Hundreds. Thousands.

For dreams in my sleeps.

For regret in these eyes.

For happiness in this life.

There is room for more.

So, just wait for a second.

I'll make room for you too.

Like I always did.

Like I always will.

A Weird life

Priya Singh

Priya Singh is born & brought up in Dewas, Madhya Pradesh .Proud daughter of her father B.N.Singh (T.I).She's completed Masters of Computer Scicncc. She is a Former Educationist, communication Trainer. She's the Co-Author of the Anthologies:-"It's all about two phase : love & hate" ,"Words From Heart", "Fierce, Fearless N Flawed" & "In the way of borehole". All are available in Amazon. Till today, She's worked in 150+ Anthologies as a Co-Author. Her writing keeps her at ease. She mostly write quotes on thoughts. She loves inspiring young minds.

Instagram id- instant__thoughts_

Mail id- scspriyasingh@gmail.com

Weird

I wish I could hold on to you,

The one with whom I shared

Laughter & little pain,

The one who has all the

Might powers to make

Me chilled again.

Eyes full of love,

Hair drenched in water,

Looking down tender skin,

Thinking what could bestow

No one is here akin.

I'm more than a stranger

Who could go through a

Darkest goals,

I'm what even you don't

Know, your spirit shivers

& calls me hay as I come

& go on my way.

A Weird life

N. Krishnaveni

N. 

Krishnaveni is an aspiring writer and a budding poet. One of her poems "My Beloved Damsel!" has published in The Literary Herald journal. She is a co-author of 'Deep Words', 'Pet Love', 'Meri YaadonKaShahar', 'A Kiss of Love', 'Chaos – Tales of Heart', 'God's Gift', 'Tales of Love', 'Paryavaran', and 'Rejoiced Life' which won the records titled as "Unique Palindrome Poetry Book" by India Book of Records and "Grand Masters" by Asia Book of Records. Most of her poems deals with the theme of nature, human emotions, and philosophical thoughts. Her poetry voices out the deepest emotions and secrets that are left unspoken and destined to be beautifully inked. Having a creative artistic propaganda, her writings hails from the articulate thoughts with coherence, spontaneity and flowery language.

Insta id: krishi_aju

SWEET AND BITTER

The hands that lift you up

In your hard and worst times

Turned as the one dug the same hole

To make you all servile and grateful to them

Throughout your whole life.

Life looks so cruel and will test you hard

In the time you desperately chase your dreams

But will surprise you with all you desire for

At the times you least expect anything

As a great reward for your perseverance and
patience.

How strange is that!

You leave someone whom you love

With all your heart deeply and sincerely,

Whom you think your happiness behind,

Cause you love them that hard.

Lalithaa S S

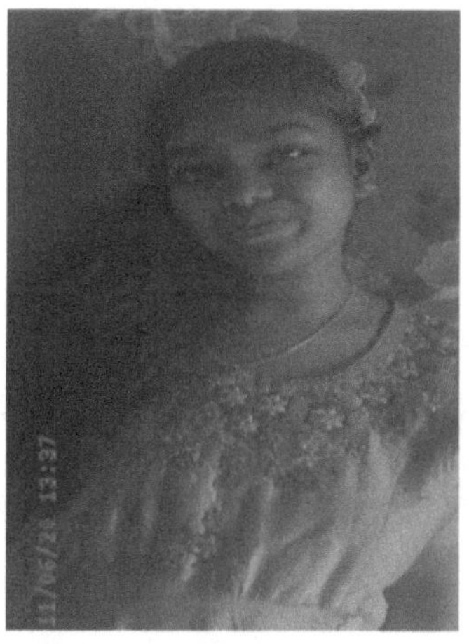

LALITHAA S S – young budding writer from Tamil Nadu. Writings makes her life more meaningful and charismatic. She is the Co compiler of ignite your soul. She has been co author of life is a chance, united by heart, bowl of cherries and so on.

Insta id: the.divine.heart

WEIRD LIFE

Life is like a sky,

There are so many stars,

But we only see the moon,

All of them writing poem about moon,

Moon disappears for somedays,

But stars are permanent,

Some people are like stars,

But we don't care about them,

We insult them,

We criticize them,

But they are still with you forever and ever,

Try to know the stars in your life,

Your life become so beautiful,

If any problem arises,

Your stars will be always there for you,

To fight for you,

Be grateful to your stars…!

Weird life…!!!

M.Srinithi

She is srinithi . She completed her master degree in English literature. She is a blogger and budding writer who written many excellent blogs and verse . She is outstanding scholar and talented woman.

Insta id: Srinithi_manoharan

Hurt....

Who hurts you?...your Friends? your love? your environment?..

It's you hurting yourself...

 They don't want you but u want them....that hurts...

You don't get nothing ,but expect...

Ur own expectation hurt you .. Not them...

They not gonna value at u..

But you crying... that hurts...

They not understand you, But u explain...

 That hurts ...

They don't want spent time with you ...

But you want them entire life with them... That hurts... Know your value... Dont blame others...

Its you, until you allow someone to hurt you ..

You not get hurt...

Ajeeba Jahan A

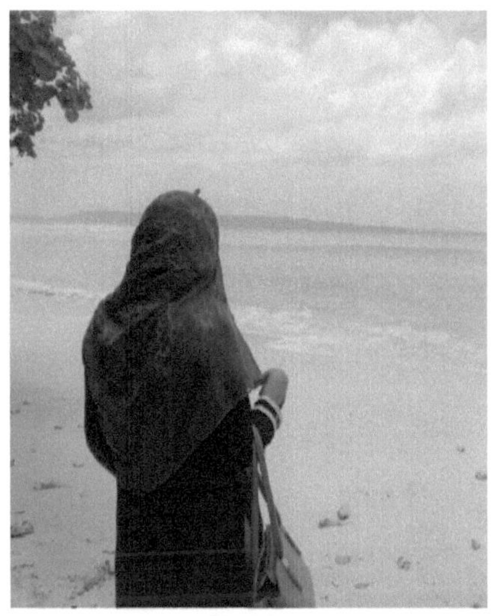

Ajeeba, a budding free verse writer.

Aspire to write more.

Avid reader.

LIES

Lie, It is a beautiful thing.

Lying is fine.

By telling, I mean necessary lies.

It is an art of convincing.

Lies are vital.

Cannot think of the world

In a Stream of Naked truth.

'I hate you, Mam' – Slap.

Lie fairly.

Maybe tell me – 'I hate your poem '.

Stay away from those

Who spews lies.

Lie within bounds.

Eventually, we all are LIARS.

73 | Page

Nirudhi N.R

Nirudhi N.R is an English Student. She is enchanting about writing poems and quotes. She has been a co-author of more than fifty anthologies. She wants to become a writer in the upcoming future. She is happy to be a part of this incredible book.

Insta id: bae_niru

INTO THE MOON.

Right, when the day goes this evening,

I research the mountains,

As tranquil as an at this point evening.

I'm the exhausting Moon.

I come to a couple of years,

I skim joyfully over mists,

Full-looked in night fall's remaining by light.

I'm the exhausting Moon.

Streak, snap, streak,

Hordes of individuals look toward me,

Like a crowd of paparazzi.

Streak, snap, streak.

I stay by perseveringly to return.

Moreover, overwhelm your night once more.

S.T. Renuka

S T Renuka, She is pursuing her BE degree,

She is Interested in reading and writing quotes, poetries, stories, drawing and exploring her Motherland INDIA and beautiful Nature♡..

TURN WEIRD TO INTERESTING

A daily routine of

Same tasks inside the home

Missing colleges and friends

Goes weird and boring !

Trying to do the daily tasks

In different manner !

But this weird routine made

The mindset bloom towards

Learning and doing some

Interesting works which will

Upgrade further days !

~ S.T. RENUKA

Mohini Keshri

She is Mohinikeshri.she is from muzaffarpur (Bihar).she is currently pursuing graduation B.sc (physics Honours). She is interested in creativity and with that she keeps a spirit in writing.she is passionate about learning.she is interested in writing short stories and poems.Her hobby is reading books.

My insta I'd is mohinikeshri26

A weird Life

No one knows what's behind a smile.

No one knows why life walks miles and miles.

No one knows why there is death after life.

No one knows why there is pain after hurt.

No one knows why there is feeling for some one in heart.

Life always gives a chance to everyone,

So accept all the challenges,

Life sometimes gives you happiness and sometimes sadness,

But don't questioned it , just accept it ,

Because everything happens for a reason.

Understand the depth of the ocean to understand the life.

It is so wonderful , you will be revived

Deeper the ocean , longer the life,

Life is a chance an opportunity to be a part of earth.

Banupriya K

She is K.Banupriya hails from Thoothukudi district. She is currently pursuing post graduate M.Sc Mathematics. She usually writes a blog. She got a medal for her service from Indian National Development and Reformation Association shortly abbreviated as INDRA TRUST.

Insta id: banu_k_11

The Smile of nature!

The smile of the sky is a rainbow!

The smile of the rainbow is color!

The smile of the tree is green!

The smile of the sun is bright light!

The smile of the moon is white!

The smile of the flower is smell!

The smile of the music is soft!

The smile of the water is pure!

The smile of the pen is letters!.

The smile of the food is delicious!

The laughter of lightning is lighten!

The laughter of thunder is loud!

All in all, Laughter is beauty.

Even more so the laughter of nature is awesome!

Vishnupriya S

Vishnupriya S MA.,M.Phil.,B.Ed., (Ph.D)., is an occasional writer. She is a zoophilist by nature with fair & square demeanor. She is an ardent fellow who tends To learn and share new things with her cronies. She relies on, 'Hope is the only light despite of all the darkness'.

You Horrendous Corona…!

Don't make people panic,

With your deadly trick.

People are almost sick,

Do depart away from the world very quick.

It took years for us to grow,

But you killed many with a single blow.

All the countries lost their glow,

And you are in a zippy flow.

144 everywhere,

Peace nowhere,

Struggling anywhere,

To live somewhere.

As you freaked,

People are locked.

We wont be anymore your prey,

And your bereavement is soon with the hope of our pray.

Stay Home, Stay Safe.

Ajitha Gulnas J

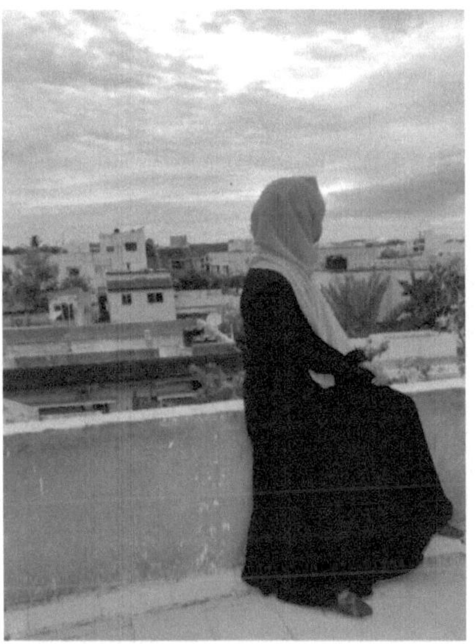

AjithaGulnas J, a 22-year-old girl, who is a budding poet, a selenophile, nature lover and a bibliophile. Her avocation is reading novels. She is a loyal and responsible person who believes in "verily with hardship, there is relief."

A Tint of Positivity

-AjithaGulnas J

When people ask, "How are you?"

Probably the answer would be "I'm fine."

But only the heart knows it's a lie.

When people ask, "How's your life?"

Probably the answer would be "Yeah it's good."

But deep inside we know it's not true.

No idea about what happened,

No idea about what is happening,

No idea about what will happen.

Amidst all the chaos around us,

Dilemmas in getting vaccinated,

Unable to resume our normal lives.

Still clinging to a tint of positivity that

Everything will be alright soon.

T R SRI VIDYA APARNA

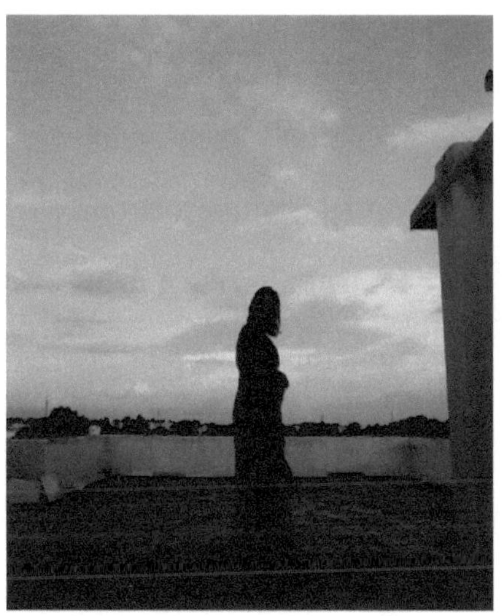

I am Sri VidyaAparna.I am a proud Indian, a literature person and an IAS Aspirant

Insta id: Aparna_Sri

MY FRIENDS

Sometimes like a Father

Sometimes like a Mother

Sometimes like a Brother

Sometimes like a Sister

Sometimes like a master

Sometimes like a monster

Sometimes like a fighter

Sometimes like a Spoiler

Sometimes like a Pointer

Sometimes like a Ladder

Sometimes like a Motivator

But always FRIENDS FOREVER

Sumathi palanisamy

She is sumathipalanisamy, pursuing her master of arts in literature. She loves to flirt with words.

She wants to express her thoughts through writings.

Insta id: Sumathi_scribbling

Failure

Made me strong

Made me give my best

Made to self motivate

Made me not step back

Made me not do the same mistake again

Made me prove myself

Made me fight for what I want

Made me not to get divert

Made me take a risk

Made me realise why can't I

Made me strong enough

Behind every success story, theirs is failure

Behind every failure, they will pay for success

Durga Balamadhavan

Durga Balamadhavan is a self-built writer & a 17 years old girl who has a kindling fire to achieve. She's a co-author of 40+ anthologies 3 world record anthologies till date & compiling her on going anthologies " The next billionaire" & "The Thirst to Travel". You can DM her in insta page @quotescumarts to get success & love quotes, poetry at a reasonable charge. Her soul finds happiness in Music, Dance, Creative Writing, Drawing & Painting…

Insta id: quotescumarts

Life – An Emotional Rollercoaster

I'm still confused what's this life meant to teach me? Most of the times, it's hitting me badly & only few moments bestow me glee.

Somedays& sometimes I could feel an emptiness in my heart And I really don't know how to figure it out?

Loved ones leave my life for no reason at all.

The moment they departed from me, my heart feels so hard. I wish to completely erase them from my mind.

But the places travelled with them throws back memories refusing their thoughts to wind.

Unexpectedly, life honours me with trophies & prizes. But at the next moment it seizes my close friends from my life as they feel much envious.

Sometimes, no matter how much I try & put in my hardwork, I'm rewarded with nothing.

But I do know, I'll succeed one day & it's a sure thing. I'm not going to search for the meaning of life anymore.

Instead, I gonna make my life meaningful & explore. Hard times do exist but they no longer persist.

Hereafter, I'd like to just embrace my life's twists.

~uniquedreamerdurga

RamadeviChelliah

Sarara is an upcoming budding writer, who shares her thoughts ,to broaden the views of people,and heal the world with her words!

Insta id: lyricist_in

Rainy drops

Oh,dew drops are falling,

My heartbeat is soring,

Birds are chirping,

My body is shivering!

With this chill weather,

My tiny fingers became feathers,

And I eat some hot chips,

To make me grip!

I want the rain each day

To make me thirst

And continue my quest!!

Kajal Chaudhary

Kajal Chaudhary is a student of grade 12 currently living in a district of Uttar Pradesh. This 17 year old girl developed an interest in writing and now she is on the path to develop it more.

Insta id: _dear_poet

Weird

There's chaos

In my

Calmness

Strength

In my

Weakness

Love

In my

Broken heart

People call me

Weird

But, there's

Naturality

In my

Weirdness

Jebisha

I am Jebisha. Writing is my Passion. I worked as a co-author in more than thirty anthologies and still working in many anthologies. I love to write poems and articles that speaks about the social issues and I love to write poems that speaks about the beauty of the nature. And this is one of the poem that speaks about the beauty of the Moon…

Insta id: jebisha.jebisha.5680

A moon walk..

The nights sometimes that scares us,

With it's darkness everywhere..,

Become more beautiful with the – shining

Of the moon and it's twinkling friends ..

I love to go for a moon walk..

I want the cool breeze to accompany me..

Both the moon and the chill cool breeze

Makes the beautiful company..

I want to relax myself forgetting all my upsets and
want to get a fresh feel..

Moon, the symbol of way in the darkness..

You guide many travelers in the dark..

You are a beauty in the dark..

I always admire your beauty..

You are an adorable one..!!

ATHIRA CK

Athira C.K resident of Kerala from malappuram district. She is Post Graduated in Plant Biotechnology .She is skilled in poetry writing and story telling. She started writing to express her thoughts from her heart. she has been a co-author in more than 25 anthologies and many more to participate also being the compiler of 3 anthologies.

Insta id: aathi_athirack

Gleam of prospect

Breeze is whispering the echoes of jeopardy

Gloom wrappes the cheek of twilight

When the consequences of human activities cover
to them

Then nature copies the colour of rainbow

The boundaries of nature leads the mankind to
move on

They are walking through summer of life realities

They swim in the torrent of crisis

After the conflict of autumn the new rays of
prospect will touch the seed

When treat the nature softly it will give birth to
spring..

ShanmugaPriya.T

ShanmugaPriya.T grew up in
Madurai,Tamilnadu,India.She is fledgling Aviator
studied in Coimbatore.She has vast fascination
pouring out her thoughts into verbal.And she
believes best companion and true ones are dogs
&books.Rather than exhibiting,she prefers
inking.She's aspiring writer and Looking forwards
for platforms.

Insta id: _ukiyo_ame_

MELANCHOLY SOUL

It's just alike another night,

Staying awake as owl

With running caprice multi mode

No clue what's wrong with me

But I do know I can't feel okay!free

It's like I'm caged in prison of cell

Where my mind is being tortured making into heart-throb & resulting in headache,

Struggling with numerous midnight crisis thoughts.

And at that day, With a smile on your face you have to survive.

-Vernita

Prachi Gupta

Prachi Gupta is a Passionate writer who loves to create her imaginary arts in a random canvas. She is pursuing her studies in BBA and lives in Allahabad known as The pure city of Sangam.

She loves to sing and watching movies in her free time. She is a shy and a open-minded girl at the same time For more information can follow her and contact:-

Prachiguptt0210@gmail.com

@prachigupta3435

@prachi_gupta_210

NO ONE CARES

Some pretend,

Some reacts

Some shows,

Some lies

Some hate, some go

Some love,

Some betrayed

Who really cares?

Some come, some shaded

Some laugh, some stay

Some hold, some leave

Throughout all these

No one really cares!!

Srijita Saha

Co-author SrijitaSaha is a good writer from Kolkata.She has Completed her.education in 12th in science stream. She has been Writing poetry for 2-3 months as her passion. She wants to be a Writer in future.

Instagram: @feel_words_of_quoetry

The unpredicted life

Life is unpredicted,

It's unprecedented.

Life has weird norms

Encourages us to eradicate all worms.

Life asks questions,

Pricks us with love infections.

Life has adventurous rules,

Makes us know our best role.

Life is not granted,

It's what every one wanted.

Life lessens our tensions,

Makes us acknowledge of our mind satisfaction.

Enjoy life, it's the road to all evens and odds.

With pride, it makes our chest broad.

K.Prathik

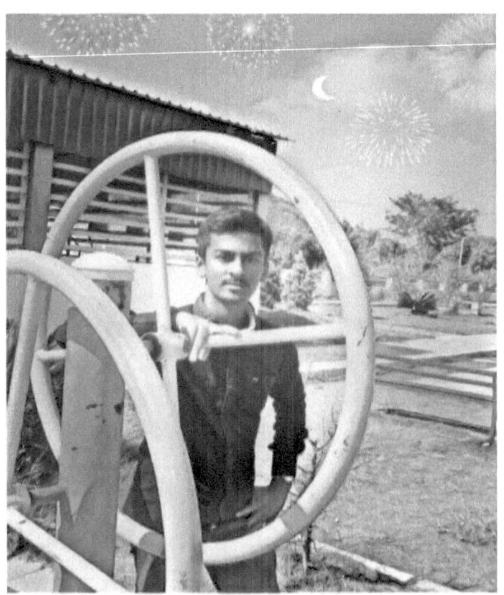

Prathik was a YouTuber with a pen name PrathikKantharaj. He was also a blogger and orator. He had participated more than 15 debates and 5 factual debates. He was a content creator and writer. Especially he loves to write Tamil and English. He has done several anthologies and done his bachelor art in Hindi. He was also a socialist and motivational speaker.

Insta id: Prathikkantharaj

Quotes

1. Use the spotlight strategy to overcome struggles that you face in your life.

2. Win or loss; if you win it is a victory, if you lose it is an experience.

3. Don't point out others, while you point them, your remaining fingers are pointing you.

4. Don't spare your enemies; win them with your brain to prove them who you are.

5. Keep on your guts, but don't let it for anyone. Be the one what you are.

Mohamed Sathik M

Mohamed Sathik M, is an Engineer by profession and a budding poet with passion who is blessed with a soft-hearted nature. He is an avid fellow one who always relies on, 'Hardwork never fails'.

Fatal Flame

Covid – 19, The name,

Which roared the world around with flame,

And soon became very fame.

The death rate of corona turned high,

People started to sigh,

And we lost our social tie.

The world turned so dark,

Wish to fly out like a lark,

And to sight back the sceneries in the park.

To go out, have to think twice,

Need to wash our hands thrice,

And a request to all, to be wise.

Raja Boovendran. P

He is Raja. He is a mechanic.

Insta id: _modifying_mechanic_offical

FIRST MEETING

I still remember our first meeting

One fine dawn

I am waiting for you

I see you at distance

My eyes searching for you

In a dark,

Your face glows like a moon

That look mesmerize me

That moment made as

You are my life

You are the light

In my darkness

A Weird life

Kousika Moorthi

KousikaMoorthi, She's a Literature Graduate currently living in Coimbatore. She had a great interest in writing from her childhood. From then till now she never stopped her imagination towards writing. She'll write about the things which affect her more and transfer her Imagination into precious words.

Insta id: solitary_diary_

WEIRD LIFE

" Thinking to write about weird is the weirdest
thing we have ever done in our life, Weird Thinking
for Weird "

" Done with my life, I can't even get up, Walk, Talk
or Eat whatever my mother Eats

All were lowering me as I am being an Infant.

Once I grew up I will sue you all for entering into
my life and decision "

" Life – does anybody know the real meaning of
Life… It tells us to fall before learning to walk,
Separate us from our favourite things to know their
true value, Madly badly gruelling us in tough
settings to appreciate our good times, Even bad
ones in our life have a meaning to be in. Does Life
mean to be Beautiful or to be Weirdest? "

Saurabh Sant Gyaneshwar Khobragade

I am SaurabhSantGyaneshwarKhobragade hailing from Chattishgarh . I started my journey of writing from the Ashes of feeling. I like to express my emotions through the medium of words and shape into shayaris and Quote. Lafz -e- dil is my first anthology as Complier and I am also written solo book of ShabadokaKalakaar and I believe that it's great achievement for me . Along with this I'm co-author of more than 25+ books and currently I am working on Promoter and you can connect me on Instagram @Srbhkhbgd @sb_talks

WEIRD LIFE

Unfaithful,

your innocent face is not capable

of putting my heart,

you are the one

whose memories

I have wasted,